Comfort for the Day

Living through the Seasons of Grief

Steve & Karen Nicola

WESTBOW
P R E S S®
A DIVISION OF THOMAS NELSON
& ZONDERVAN

ISBN: 978-1-4497-1881-7 (e)
ISBN: 978-1-4497-1882-4 (sc)

Library of Congress Control Number: 2011931477

WestBow Press books may be ordered through booksellers or by contacting:

WestBow Press
A Division of Thomas Nelson & Zondervan
1663 Liberty Drive
Bloomington, IN 47403
www.westbowpress.com
844-714-3454

Printed in the United States of America.

WestBow Press rev. date: 09/28/2020

❦ Contents ❧

∞ ─── ᘓ

Dear Reader ﻬ

    The night was long, but not long enough. How we wished we could travel back in time just three short months. Our precious first born son, Dawson, was in remission then, and our little daughter, Joanna, played contentedly with her "big" brother. We were a very happy family of four. If only we could hold those cherished days in a timeless bottle . . . But there is no such opportunity.

    The night was dark and the morning grew darker as we pressed ourselves nearer to Dawson's bed. Just at sunrise our son lost his battle with leukemia. There are no words. You know that. While Leukemia had won, the love in our hearts has never been overtaken by suffering or time.

Steve: Each morning I woke, it felt like I was a freight train slamming into a brick wall.

Karen: I couldn't cry easily with others.

Steve: I wanted to talk about my son and his death to anyone who would listen.

Karen: It felt like I would never come back from my journey into grief.

Together: We trusted God to help us.

    Our loss is not a model for you. We do not share our story to add to your pain. We just want you to know that our hearts beat in the rhythm of pain with yours. We want you to know what brought healing for our broken hearts is available for you too. If your wife lingered in a painful death, if your parent has recently passed away, if your husband died suddenly, if your child was killed by a drunk driver, or if a sibling recently took his own life, this book is written for you.

    We look forward to being supportive friends as you live through the seasons of your grief. ﻬ

Steve & Karen

❧ How to Use This Book ❧

You are hurting. Right now the pain is unlike anything you have experienced. Words like "arrangements," "process," "stages," and "grief" may cause you to recoil and insist this is all a bad dream. Even reading can seem insurmountable. For that reason, this grief recovery guide is designed for your unique, broken hearted needs. Our intention is that you find comfort here as you move through your individual seasons of grief.

Why should I use this book?

That's a great question. Why should you read a book about your grief? What can this book do for you? Comfort for the Day is an intentionally crafted grief recovery journal. It gives you, the reader, a place to practice healthy grieving, be honest with your feelings and experience God's comfort for each day of sorrow. This means . . .

- o You have a safe place to express your deepest feelings
- o You can be assured that God is personally interested in your suffering
- o You can be encouraged that you are moving forward in your healing.
- o You can see how God helps to clear up confusion as you reread your entries
- o You can be less concerned with unanswered questions
- o You can be comforted that you are not alone in your pain.

Accept Your Individuality

Your loss is unique and only you know your pain. Each "Comfort for the Day" was written to stimulate your mind, encourage you to absorb God's care, comfort, and, most importantly, provide a cushion for your pain. Grief recovery is different for everyone because male, female, parent, child, grandparent, and friend will face the loss uniquely. We need comfort and support, encouragement and understanding; as well as to become aware of our own responses and reactions to our private sorrow.

Emotional and Physical Side Effects of Grieving

The following sections in this book, "Comfort for Your Emotional Grief" and "Understanding Your Physical Grief," will support you as you learn about common grief experiences. The fear of the unknown is an added stress that you do not need. Therefore, becoming acquainted with the physical side effects and emotional aspects of grief will help reduce your fear and provide you with a more relaxed state of mind, which promotes healing.

Begin Anywhere

This book is *not* a "start-to-finish" book. This is *not* a coffee table book, or library shelf book. This is *not* a workbook. *This is a safe place to be real with your sorrow.* It is an opportunity to encounter God's comfort and never ending love. It is a book you can open and read in any section to find encouragement, information, and help. It is a book to use. Write in it, draw in it, and jot down notes, poetry, quotes, and favorite memories. Skim through the pages and find a title or section that resonates with your need at the moment. These pages will become your personalized grief recovery story. We believe we never *get over* the loss, but rather we heal, and our healing progresses throughout the seasons of our lives. Therefore, this book is intended to be useful for as long as you continue to heal and discover the importance of writing to express your process.

Write On, Put Your Stuff on Paper

You do not need to consider yourself a writer. Healing work does not require previous writing skills. You have thoughts and feelings; just put those on paper. No order, structure, or rules are needed. Grief is messy, unpredictable and random. Putting your stuff on paper is going to reflect the messy random, unpredictable experiences you are facing. If you write to God, it is like praying on paper. You can tell Him everything. Jotting down your feelings clarifies the grief process and helps promote lasting healing. Using this book as a tool begins the opportunity for healing that will help you move through your pain. As a result, you might find yourself strengthened to face the reality of your varied emotions as they come day by day ~ one season at a time.

Built-up grief is like poison in your system that needs to be released. Express that grief on paper, and your mind and body will begin to heal. As you put pen to paper, do not feel that you must fill the entire page. However, once you begin expressing these thoughts or feelings, you may surprise yourself. Use the extra pages at the back of the book to continue. Your jumbled thoughts scratched out on paper will help the tension subside. Dating your entries may help you as you return to any of the "Comforts" many weeks or months later to record additional thoughts. If you prefer to sketch your thoughts and feelings, by all means use that talent to release your emotions. You will find drawing pages near the end of this book.

Men and Journaling ~ *Steve's Perspective*

Let's face it men, when it comes to communicating our thoughts on paper, there is something that prevents many of us from seeing the value in doing it. If you are among many men who look at journaling as a type of "Dear Diary" then let me assure you it is not. I remember writing my first good-bye letter to my son, not long after he died. I was surprised by the tears that came so easily as I wrote. I was also surprised at how much better I felt after I was finished. It brought a sense of relief. I believe that when men are willing to write we will discover a new way of tapping into our deepest emotions.

I have a good friend who has journaled since he was a teen. He explains his journaling experience this way: *"Journaling has taken many forms, including; daily notations in a small calendar, written reflections in a pocket New Testament, typing my prayers on my laptop, pouring out my heart to God on paper as I anguished with some life crisis or thorny issue, and making notes on my Outlook Calendar reminding me to pray for others or give thanks to God. Always, writing my thoughts solidifies and often clarifies them for me. Reading them later can inspire me with God's progressive work in my life. There is something tangible and confirming about reading later what was written with such passion, confusion, frustration or joy. Journaling is simply another way to more clearly listen and speak to God."* Doug Tilstra

Men, the fact that you are reading this says you are serious about your grief and healing from your loss. We have so much to gain when we do, and much to lose if we do not track our process through this journey called grief.

The Comfort of Scripture

The last pages of this book have additional Scripture verses. On those days when you need extra support and comfort, turn to these pages to easily find a text from Scripture that will speak to your need for the moment. Because our God is the "God of all comfort" (2 Corinthians 1:3), His Word is filled with the comfort you need right now. These Scriptures helped us find solace and comfort throughout the stressful seasons of our emotional and physical grief seasons. We hope they will do the same for you.

Make Your Own Adjustments

While we have been intentional to write in a way that will allow for a broad spectrum of death and grieving experiences, it will happen that some of the ideas expressed might not match your experience. It is our desire that you, the reader, make adjustments to fit your needs, incorporating what works and setting aside what doesn't.

Our Prayer

We encourage you to put your trust in God. He loves you and wants to be intimately involved in your healing. Our prayer is that *Comfort for the Day* will become a welcomed companion as you live through your seasons of grief. We pray that the thoughts and emotions penned in this guided journal will contribute to your personal healing journey.

"Lord, please give this broken hearted reader the comfort and healing he or she needs for each day."

Confident in God's Faithfulness to Heal,

~ Steve & Karen ~

Comfort for Your Emotional Grief

"You have searched me, Lord, and you know me …
You perceive my thoughts from afar."
Psalm 139:1–2 NKJV

What a comfort to remember that our God knows us each individually. Just as each of us is unique, so will be our pain. No two grief experiences are alike. Several emotional phases of recovery will be part of your experience. Knowing what the different experiences could be for you will give you relief as you pass through them, often many times over. Generally, most people who are experiencing grief focus on the loss, experience a season of depression, followed by hope, and eventually adjustment. A hospital chaplain, once told us, "Grieve when you grieve, and when you don't grieve, don't grieve." Sounds simple! But accepting our varied emotions and feelings during the seasons of grief can be a difficult task.

Seasons of Grief

It might be helpful to know that many words are used to describe the experiences of grieving. We refer to them as seasons. May I remind you that just as seasons are interrupted with brief unexpected interludes of diverse weather patterns; likewise, our grieving is even less predictable. However, knowing what others have experienced can help diminish the fear we may feel when emotional storms assail. Here is a list of emotional experiences we have compiled. You may or may not experience all of these, but when you do, please be assured that these are only grief's seasons and they will pass.

Shock	Numbness	Despair
Denial	Panic	Blame
Hurt	Depression	Loneliness
Regrets	Relief	Anxiety
Guilt	Fear	Loss of emotional control

Anger	Hostility	Socially awkward
Acceptance	Hopeful	Reconciliation
_____	_____	_____

Healthy Grieving

After loss everyone grieves. Our loss will affect us for the remainder of our lives. The question we need to ask ourselves is: Do I want this grief to leave me less of a person or help me become better? If you were to injure your arm, either with a broken bone or torn rotator cuff, would you get medical attention? Of course! You would even endure additional pain to set the bone so your arm could be functional again. Going to physical therapy after a rotator cuff surgery would also be painful, but you would choose to do it because you know it is part of the healing process so your arm could regain its usefulness.

When we suffer with a broken heart, it is often hidden from others. Our culture suggests that we just "get on with our lives." There is little encouragement to attend to the pain and even less encouragement to accept there will be pain as our broken heart goes through its healing process. Healing broken hearts doesn't happen automatically, just like healing a broken bone doesn't happen unattended. We call healthy grieving, grief work. It is demonstrated when we admit we need to grieve and that grief work is difficult, but it is the very thing needed to heal. Attending to our grief through actively journaling, participating in grief support with others, reading, and preparing for significant dates are all part of healthy grief. We often refer to it as our grief work. It is something we intentionally choose, just like choosing to participate in physical therapy exercises. The result is healthy grief.

> "The only cure for grief is to grieve." Earl Grollman

Grief's Staircase

The grief work process is very much like climbing stairs. Imagine yourself climbing one of the world's famous stairways, some as short a 100 steps and others 3700 steps long. While climbing, you might observe others treading slowly, some more rapidly, and still others taking several steps at a time. When it comes to grief, do not allow yourself to compare your grief to another's. Remember, you are unique, and your grief work will be unique to fit your needs and personality. You may find that your "stair-stepping" experience will take you back down one or more steps during difficult moments. Then you may find yourself ascending several steps at a time. Some steps must be climbed over and over again, but more healing takes place each time you climb that emotional step.

Waves of Grief

It is very difficult to anticipate the varying emotions of grief; however, denying or running from those emotions will only prolong the recovery process. Grieving emotions can be compared to waves on the beach. We know that waves continually break against the ocean's shore, yet it is difficult to anticipate their size and force. Intense emotions can come upon us in the most unexpected places and during the most unexpected times. Ten years after Dawson died I remember silently crying in the middle of a meeting at a women's retreat. Out of nowhere, sadness overtook me, and the tears spilled out.

A sneaker wave (larger and more forceful than other waves) at the ocean can at times move more quickly than we can outrun. Sometimes the wave even trips us and we fall. Likewise, running from our emotions can leave us emotionally "tripped up." Face the wave. Face the emotions head-on.

After you have faced your feelings honestly, you can acknowledge them. These experiences are benchmarks in your recovery. Don't fight, don't resist, and don't struggle. Allow the wave of emotion to hit. Give yourself permission to float in the feelings for a time. During that time, reason with yourself about what the reality of the situation is versus your emotions. As you spend this time weighing the truth as you know it against your emotions, you will discover the freedom to accept your emotions and the freedom to give them up to the sea, allowing your reason to bring you back to shore and reality.

As I wept that afternoon, I realized that my love for our son would ever be present. I was encouraged to know that pain was not my enemy, but rather a reminder of my love.

> While feelings are real, they are not reality K. Nicola

Through it all, trusting God with the timing and assurance of His healing will help put you back on your feet again. Never does the cry for God's help go unheeded. He is anxious to bring you the help you need. He is your best source of support for all your grieving experiences.

Anger: An Unsettling Reality

Death is a hard hitting loss of control. This often expresses itself through anger. Many find themselves surprised with angry emotions. We would be extremely reluctant to admit to anyone that we are angry at the one who just died and/or at God.

It was a warm afternoon. Our daughter wasn't napping. I was frustrated. No! Actually, I was angry. So after the 4th or 5th time I put her back into her crib, I went to my own bed and started to journal. I wrote that I was angry at little Joanna for not napping. I was angry at Steve for going back to work. I was angry at Dawson for dying and leaving me in such pain. I was angry at God. After spending sometime releasing my feelings on paper, I found I could step back into the mothering demands of my day. (By the way, Joanna remained in her crib and finally napped.)

Anger is a normal part of grief, but for most of us, it is unsettling. It is during this time that facing our emotions as an ocean wave becomes a useful grief recovery tool. Face the anger. Accept the feeling as a part of grief. Float with the anger, reasoning what is true about the love of God versus how we *feel*. Then humbly ask God to let our anger go out to sea; trusting His love to bring us back to shore in His healing embrace. I think the most important idea I want you to know is that God is bigger than our anger. We can beat on his chest with all our fury and still he loves and understands us. Our part is to be honest and find healthy, safe releases for our anger, such as expressing ourselves on paper or talking with a trusted person.

Learn from Others

There are several practical things you can do that will help your emotional recovery. Joining a support group is often a good way to find encouragement. Many times just listening to others and making application for your own experience can feel comforting. If the group is guided by a qualified facilitator, your experience will be very useful for you.

Reading is another way you can acquaint yourself with a deeper awareness of grief and the process of healing and recovery. By learning about others' experiences and thoughts, you have additional information to affirm your own emotions and healing. Not all things others have experienced fit every need, so trust God's Spirit for discernment. Additional comfort and encouragement can be found at www.comfortfortheday.com

Express Yourself

Putting your emotions and thoughts on paper is one of the best grief work activities that men, women, and children can do. It is a free tool that brings relief, clarity and healing for our broken hearts. This book is obviously designed to encourage your writing. Having an outlet to express your thoughts and emotions is part of the therapy for heart healing. It can be painful, but it will lead you towards healthy grieving. It is difficult for two things to occupy the same space. When we are filled with grieving thoughts and feelings, it is difficult for healing thoughts and feelings to take occupation of our minds. Write on and on until you find emotional transitions taking place inside of you. It really does work.

One of the very best, but most painful tasks we completed was to write a "good-bye" letter to our son. However, as we wrote we experienced new space in our emotions to begin to accept comfort and healing. Writing a "goodbye" letter becomes a tool for releasing all that we wish we could have said, but didn't. You may feel a deep need to express your love. A "Good-Bye" letter begins the process of accepting the interruption of the relationship, while allowing you to retain the precious or treasured memories of that relationship.

When you need to express regret, ask for forgiveness, or give forgiveness see page 36-42 for detailed steps in this kind of letter writing. A "Forgiveness" letter can do nothing to reverse the loss, but it is a necessary step toward bringing you freedom from an endless cycle of pain, guilt, and regret.

> To the degree you engage in your grief work, you will experience more or less healing. *K.Nicola*

Counseling

Seeing a good, qualified Christian counselor or Grief Coach is another tool that will aid in your emotional understanding of grief and recovery. Some people shy away from counseling because they feel it shows weakness or a lack of faith. We wouldn't avoid going to a doctor to set a broken leg. Likewise, visiting a counselor makes sense when it comes to our broken heart. A good counselor will give you emotional tools to help you process your grief. Even if your grief work is progressing well, it is advisable to touch base with a professional counselor to affirm your recovery and healing experience.

Music

Music can be a pacifier or magnifier of our emotions. It helps open us to how we really feel and can soothe the pain. Saul, the first king of Israel, often suffered from emotional distress. During these times, he would call for David to play his harp which soothed, comforted and healed his emotional disruptions. Tastes in music vary considerably, but may we suggest that during this time of emotional stress you consider listening to sacred or inspirational music. It helps to keep your focus on the realities of God and His love. It also offers hope for your broken heart.

Hobbies

As you look around your home, you may discover other emotional tools such as painting, fishing, golfing, biking, hiking, sports, yard work, hobbies or volunteering for a local charity. Participating in these activities can become a welcome relief from the ever present pain. Use this space to jot down a few activities that you could use as a respite from your pain.

_____

_____

> God is faithful to bring beauty of
> character from the ashes of our pain. K. Nicola

Please keep in mind that healthy grieving allows for periods of relief, yet continues the conscious choice to face the pain and work it through. As you come to understand your seasons of grief, your ebbs and flow of the waves of emotions, or your particular way of climbing grief stairs, you may discover a pattern that works for you. You might be aware of a deeper sense of your true self. You might discover that you are being lead in your healing towards becoming the person God is recreating you to be. This Scripture helped us keep our grief work in perspective.

> "For our light affliction, which is but for a moment, is working for us a far more exceeding and eternal weight of glory; while we do not look at the things which are seen, but at the things which are not seen. For the things which are seen are temporary but the things which are not seen are eternal." 2 Corinthians 4:17–18 KJV

While it might seem difficult at first to say that day-to-day living without our loved one is a "light affliction," in the perspective of eternity ~ in the new Heaven and new Earth ~ this season of grief will be but a speck on our whole life story. Sometimes it helps to put our pain into eternal perspective. It encourages us to see our pain as temporary and the hope of eternal realities as everlasting.

A Bereavement Spiral

Visually, grief does not resolve itself on a straight line. A better way to understand our diverse grief experiences is this spiral. It is a visual way to grasp what we are experiencing. Begin from the center. What do you notice? The intensity in early grief lessens as repetition, time, forgiveness and acceptance promotes healing.

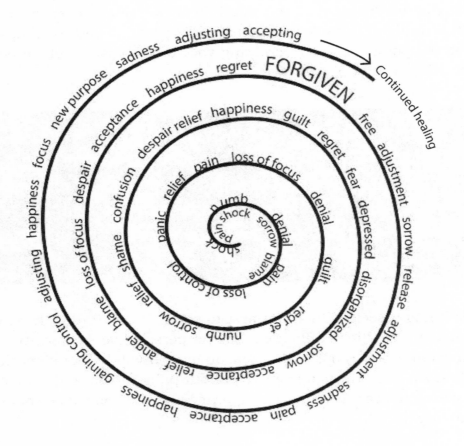

© CfD May 2016

The common "5 Stages of Grief" really best apply to the dying. A Grief Spiral is a better illustration for those of us who remain.

Acceptance	Guilt	Panic
Anger	Hopeful	Reconciliation
Anxiety	Hostility	Regrets
Blame	Hurt	Relief
Denial	Loneliness	Shock
Depression	Longing	Socially awkward
Despair	Loss of emotional control	
Fear	Numbness	

Use the blank spiral and the word bank to record your experiences. This step is part of healthy grief work and will give you hope and assurance as you face new and reoccurring emotional responses to your pain. See p. 36-42 to guide you with your forgiveness process *before* putting **FORGIVEN** on the spiral.

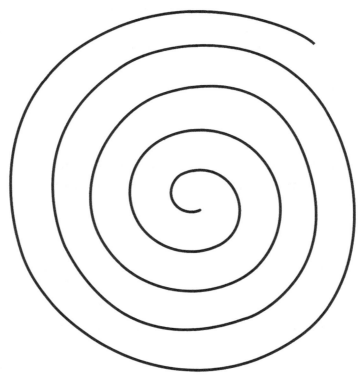

Understanding Your Physical Grief

"I praise you because I am fearfully and wonderfully made;
Your works are wonderful, I know that full well."
Psalm 139:14 TNIV

It's difficult enough to wake up to our broken hearts each morning, but our grief also has physical side effects. Since there are seldom times that ignorance is beneficial, we must inform you that of all the areas we lose control after loss, we can gain control in how we treat our bodies during our seasons of grief. Our bodies suffer from the emotional trauma and when we are unaware that it is related to our grieving, we can become quite concerned about a sudden decline in health. In this section, you will discover many ways the body is affected by our grief, shock, loss and pain. You will also be encouraged to take personal control over your body with some very simple and useful suggestions.

Weakened Immunity

First off, the immune system of the bereaved is affected by the shock and will not return to optimum capacity for up to 12 months. This is because it takes a year to encounter most of the major "firsts" without the person who died. As we move through the seasons of grief during the first year, we re-encounter deep sadness and pain.

While the heart is grieving, so is the body. Beginning each day with a good hot and then cold shower is an excellent way to get your blood circulating and mind functioning more clearly. Another benefit is that it also increases our white blood cell count which helps to fight disease, thus reducing the risk of illness.

During the first year of grief I, Karen, finished each shower with a cold rinse. No, it didn't feel great, but I figured it could be the worst thing that might happen to me that day and I had already gotten through it. I know the benefits of a cold rinse were far better than being physically sick and emotionally weak at the same time. Becoming ill only adds to our emotional grief, making it so much harder to bear, and we need all the advantages we can get.

So stay healthy! Here are a few ideas to consider:

- Avoid contact with those who are ill or contagious
- Take supplemental vitamins to increase your defense against germs
- Get plenty of rest
- Be vigilant about hand washing
- Other ways I stay healthy _____

Mental Cloud

Most noticeably, many mourners agree that they experience mental confusion, lack of focus, and an inability to make decisions or think clearly. The stress of the emotional impact weighs heavily on our mental capacity. Be kind to your mind. It has undergone an enormous amount of stress to begin processing the reality of your loss. Please consider implementing these following suggestions:

- Avoid or limit driving for the first several weeks—your lack of focus can make you a distracted driver
- Ask for assistance with bill paying
- Get plenty of rest (8 + hours/night)
- Defer major decisions for up to a year if possible
- Ask for and consider advice from trusted friends or family before making a big decision
- Other ways I help my mind _____

The Grieving Body

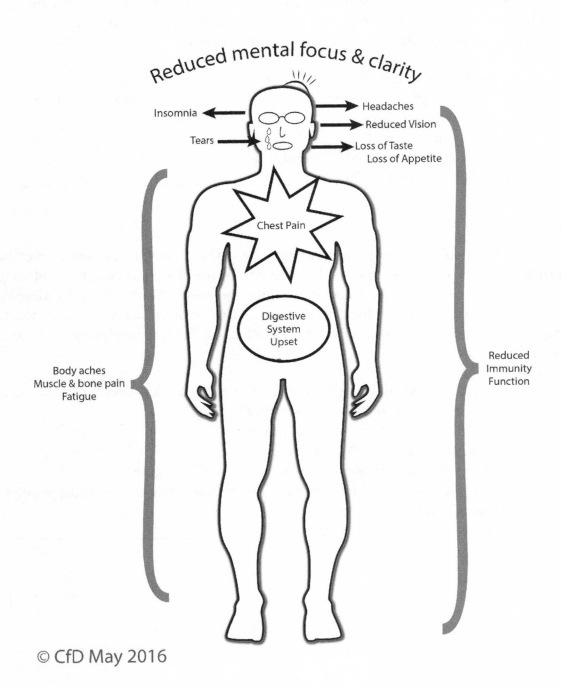

Reduced mental focus & clarity

Insomnia

Tears

Headaches

Reduced Vision

Loss of Taste
Loss of Appetite

Chest Pain

Digestive
System
Upset

Body aches
Muscle & bone pain
Fatigue

Reduced
Immunity
Function

© CfD May 2016

Physical Grief

As you look at the illustration, you will notice that many parts of the body are affected by your grief. The emotional energy that is necessary to begin to process the loss is so great that, although you have not done any physical exercises you may feel exhausted. Your entire body may experience pain in nearly every muscle. You might feel intense chest pain. Headaches are common. What can you do to gain control over your physical pain?

- o Naps and plenty of rest
- o Some added vitamins can help with fatigue and muscle pain
- o Get a massage
- o Try a warm bath or hot tub
- o Take a walk
- o Practice deep breathing or focused breathing
- o Hard physical work/exercise
- o Other ideas that work for me _____

The Digestive System

It is not surprising that the digestive system of a grieving person is in severe stress. You might experience a loss of appetite, nausea, reduction of taste bud function, over eating (seeking comfort in food), or under eating. Going without meals signals to our body that it is in an emergency and this causes imbalance. Here is what helps:

- o Eat regular small meals of easily digested food
- o Remember that grieving is hard work and needs to be fueled with nutritious calories such as whole grains, nuts, and unprocessed foods
- o Even though you don't taste food like you used to, your taste bud function will return
- o Keep some dried fruit, crackers or nuts handy for a healthy snack
- o Avoid spicy and high sugar foods and drinks
- o Other tips that work for me _____

Steps to Regaining Physical Health

Be proactive with these eight, uncomplicated, healthy choices:

1. **A healthy diet**. Today's nutritionists recommend a diet high in fresh fruits, whole grains, fresh vegetables, and low in fat, protein, and sugar.

2. **Daily exposure to the sunshine**. The warmth of just fifteen minutes a day in the sunshine (when available) is soothing medicine to the nervous system.

3. **Lots of fresh air**. Deep breathing exercises will increase the oxygen that is needed for mental clarity. Slow rhythmic breathing that uses the abdominal muscles for inhaling and exhaling will act as a natural tranquilizer, relaxing all the muscles of the body.

4. **Daily exercise**. If you walk, jog, or garden, you will accomplish numbers two, three, and four all at one time. Physical activity promotes emotional well-being.

5. **Say "NO" to harmful substances**. Choosing to eliminate alcohol, tobacco, drugs, caffeine, and high-sugar foods will benefit your body at this critical time. The mental "food" you take in is as important as the physical, therefore consider leaving aside violent and highly emotionally charged movies, video games, and books.

6. **Lots of water**. Drink an abundance of water—no less than eight glasses of water each day. Use hot and cold showers to get you going in the morning. Experiment with a relaxing bath or shower in the evening for better rest through the night.

7. **Regular rest**. A regular routine will be a natural sleep aid. Meditation, prayer, and Bible reading can relax your physical system so your sleep is less interrupted.

8. **Trust God.** A spiritual dependence on God maximizes all healthy choices. Trusting God moment by moment of each day will provide release for all the anxieties that seek to control you. Fear, worry, anger, and depression will each find their remedy in the faithfulness of God. He alone is able to bring peace.

Tears

Even our eyes suffer due to our broken hearts. You might find that your vision is diminished for a season. Usually it only lasts a few weeks. Keep this in mind before you get a new prescription for glasses. But the most important physiological reaction to the pain of loss comes through our tears.

> "The sorrow which has no vent for tears may make other organs weep." *Henry Maudsley*

I find profound wisdom in this sentimental thought. When we swallow our tears, we are taking back into our body, something that was meant to be released. According to modern research, tears of grief actually carry body toxins that need to be eliminated.

- Allow your tears
- When tempted to swallow hard and hold in your tears, remember you are healthier for crying
- If others seem uncomfortable with your tears, let them know you are cooperating to bring healing for your broken heart by crying
- Get plenty of rest

> Those who sow with tears will reap with songs of joy. *Ps. 126:5*

A Man's Perspective on Tears

Men grieve differently than women do. Women generally are more verbal about how they are feeling and they can give way to tears more easily than most men. If shedding tears seems to be difficult, may I suggest that writing can be a very effective means of unlocking those pent up tear ducts? I was surprised by the tears that so quickly flowed as I have written several "good bye" letters to my son over the years. Each time, after the tears, I feel relieved. King David once penned, "My soul weeps because of grief. Strengthen me according to your word." Psalms 119:28. Men, I am here to let you know it's okay to cry. It is healthy to cry. It is healing. ~ *Steve*

> "There is a sacredness in tears. They are not the mark of weakness, but of power. They speak more eloquently than a thousand tongues. They are the messengers of overwhelming grief and unspeakable love." *Washington Irving*

David, the Psalm writer, once wrote, "He heals the brokenhearted and binds up their wounds" (Psalm 147:3) TNIV. God is responsible for your healing and recovery. As you discover the advantages of cooperating with Him in your choices for your physical care, you will also enjoy His emotional and spiritual recovery more consistently and completely. Reading the suggestions in this book is one thing, but actually doing them is another. What is the risk of trying them yourself? You have nothing to lose and everything to gain.

My Plan to Incorporate These Ideas

_____

_____

_____

_____

_____

_____

_____

_____

Questions of Pain ❦ Answers of Comfort

Comfort for the Day

Comfort Available 24/7

And surely I am with you always.

Matthew 28:20

Comfort for our grief comes in different ways at different times. Comfort can be arms to hold us, a card that encourages, a visit from a caring friend, a phone call that conveys care and support, even a stranger who offers time to listen. But then there are those moments that overwhelm us in the dark. We are alone, feeling vulnerable, fragile and crushed. Who is there then? The One who has promised to never leave us or forsake us is on duty 24/7. God is our most faithful source of comfort. The Father, Jesus and the Spirit offer to comfort us. Never is there a season in our grief that God is absent, unaware or unavailable to comfort us.

From Heart to Hand

Reread any notes or cards you have received.
Write about a time you felt comforted.
Write a prayer asking God to help you become aware of His comfort.

Picture God's Comfort

This is why I weep and my eyes overflow with tears. No one is near to comfort me, no one to restore my spirit.

Lamentations 1:16 TNIV

As a mother comforts her child, so will I comfort you; and you will be comforted.

Isaiah 66:13 TNIV

℞_____℟

Some of us might find it challenging to receive comfort from a Divine or Supernatural Being. May I suggest putting into practice a bit of active imagination. Wherever you are right now, picture the presence of God with you in your room. He might be sitting next to you with his arm around your shoulder, or you might see yourself enfolded in a full embrace of motherly love and tenderness. God could be sitting opposite from you, leaning forward, listening to all your breaking heart has to say. Envision a tender hand wiping your tears and crying along with you. The One who loves you most can be trusted to be the most faithful comforting presence. Just allow it to be so.

℞_____℟

From Heart to Hand

Write about how you imagine God comforting you.
Write a letter to God thanking Him for His comforting presence.
Make a list of comforting Scripture verses. (see pages 148-149)

God Loves You

Who shall separate us from the love of Christ? Shall trouble or hardship or persecution or famine or nakedness or danger or sword? For I am convinced that neither death nor life, neither angels nor demons, neither the present nor the future, nor any powers, neither height nor depth, nor anything else in all creation, will be able to separate us from the love of God that is in Christ Jesus our Lord.

Romans 8:35, 38–39 TNIV

God's love for you has not grown cold because your heart is broken. Rather, because your heart is crushed, His compassion and tenderness is all the more directed toward you. Your great need can assure you of His even greater, more abundant supply. You may not always *feel* His unconditional love for you, but you can rest in the *knowledge* of His love. God's unconditional love for you is found throughout His word and in the living witness of His Son, Jesus. Nothing can separate you from His love. Cling to the knowledge of God's love, regardless of how you feel. Your emotions cannot be trusted during grief, but you can trust God's word in the Bible when He says that nothing can separate you from His love. Allow this assurance of God's limitless love to hold you as you face the painful days ahead.

From Heart to Hand

What evidence of God's eternal love for me have I experienced today?
When I don't _feel_ God's love, how does this Scripture assure me?
How can trusting God's word about His love help my pain today?

Meet Your Heart Specialist

He heals the brokenhearted and bandages their wounds.

Psalm 147:3 TNIV

God takes complete responsibility for comforting and healing your broken heart. Through Jesus, He has become a *man* acquainted with grief. Yet, have you ever stopped to think that He is also *God* acquainted with grief? As infinite as Divinity is, so is His capacity to feel hurt and pain. His pain is so much greater than ours could ever be for He is aware of and feels the pain of every human situation. He knows and understands. Most of all, He alone can heal. It is just as much a miracle today to see a person recover from their loss as it was to see the lame walk and the blind see in the days of Jesus' earthly ministry. May you trust your heavenly Cardiologist today. He will provide the remedies and bandages of hope, forgiveness, peace, and assurance of His never ending presence with you.

From Heart to Hand

What can I do to cooperate with my heavenly Physician?
Reflect on how God must feel as He shares in humanity's pain.
What kind of "bandages" is God applying to my grief process?

Mental Pictures

We take captive every thought to make it obedient to Christ.

II Corinthians 10:5

Death often leaves hideous, unforgettable pictures in our minds ~ either imagined or real. The question is; do these images promote my recovery and well-being or do they trap me on an endless wheel of suffering? At times like these, grief work needs to become very focused and intentional. Choosing to take mental action by practicing the wisdom found in the above Scripture is necessary to bring relief from the horrifying images that uncontrollably appear on your mental screen. The reality is that we have many more pleasant mental images of our loved one. On days like these it requires our intentional choice to discard the pain-filled image and replace it with one that is beautiful, cherished, loved, and positive. You might need to work with this process frequently. The trauma of death is not quickly remedied. Yet, by practicing healthy grieving tools, the hurtful images will subside, leaving the positive ones prominent in your thinking.

Heart to Hand

Write a plan of what you will do to exchange
hurtful images of your loved one with better ones.
Write your treasured or favorite scenes you hold in your mind's eye.
Sketch something that is a positive image of
your loved one. (see Sketch pages)

He Can Be Trusted

You will keep in perfect peace those whose minds are steadfast, because they trust in you. Trust in the LORD forever, for the LORD, the LORD, is the Rock eternal.

Isaiah 26:3–4 TNIV

If we are unfaithful, he remains faithful, for he cannot deny who he is.

2 Timothy 2:13 NLT

After all other options are weighed, who can we trust if we cannot trust God? There is no one! God is the only trustworthy friend we have. And what a friend we have in Him! We are challenged to trust someone we do not see, but He has given us abundant evidence of His trustworthiness. Whether we choose to trust Him or not, He will remain trustworthy for He cannot go against His own character. The result of trusting God with our loss and pain is peace. Peace amid loss can be gained in no other way. May you discover a new peace today as you trust God. May your peace grow as you accept His trustworthiness toward you.

From Heart to Hand

What areas of pain in my life do I need to entrust to God today?
What kind of a picture can I use to develop greater trust in God?
How can I trust Him to be faithful to me and to meet my needs right now?

Forgiveness Begins The Healing

If we confess our sins, he is faithful and just and will forgive us our sins and purify us from all unrighteousness.

1 John 1:9 TNIV

ଓଃ_____ ଓ

First, it is useful to remind ourselves that no human relationship has ever been perfect. We will each have a greater or lesser amount of unfinished business between us and the important person/s who has died. The more we remain ignorant or unwilling to deal with our regrets, the more intense we will suffer in our grief and the longer our pain will last.

Part of the cycle of grieving is the reoccurring sense of regret. This can take the shape of rehearsing the "What ifs," "If onlys," or "Wish I would have, could have, or should have." When death occurs, there remains unfinished conversations. We wish we could change those memories that haunt us. We struggle with blame and/or regrets as if in a boxing match. It might seem like we are left holding the bag of deeply painful memories. What can a brokenhearted person do to break the cycle of self-doubt, regret, guilt and blame that leaves us emotionally in shreds?

The other side of the same coin is the nagging pain that the deceased will never be able to take responsibility for the pain and hurt they caused in our lives. The unresolved conflict settles in like an ever present pebble in our shoe. What can be done? In some death occurrences, there can be cause for blaming the death on others due to malpractice, violence, substance abuse, neglect, etc.

Following WWII the German city of Berlin was divided with a high wall, complete with barbed wire and guards in watch towers to shoot anyone attempting to cross over. On the west side, residents enjoyed the freedoms of a democratic government. On the east side, people lived under the fearful, oppressive control of communism. When we do not understand and **accept** forgiveness; or when we find it impossible to **give** forgiveness, it is like living on the eastern side of the Berlin Wall. We have just set up residence in the side of the city that is dominated by fear and restrictions. This emotional state keeps us trapped in a cycle of pain. The Good News is that through the life and death of Jesus, He has broken down the wall of shame, guilt, regret, and blame. We can live free by allowing His forgiveness to heal our hearts and then freely offer this forgiveness to others.

So there is hope! What has seemed impossible to heal ourselves is completely possible to heal with God. His plan for our healing is to start with forgiveness. Accepting His great gift of forgiveness is within everyone's reach. God's forgiveness for our mistakes, dysfunctional relationships and regrets is the remedy we need for our grieving aching hearts. To the degree you, grieving reader, engage with these healing activities will be to the degree your heart will become free from the unresolved pain that may have you trapped in fear, restriction and anger.

What is Forgiveness?

Would you consider along with us that forgiveness originates with God? He is forgiveness. His attitude and character is to forgive. We need not beg, plead or twist his arm to forgive us. Before we even knew we needed forgiveness, Jesus died to become the fully authorized Forgiver of all human offense. Repeatedly, Scripture tells us that God is ready to pardon, has the right to forgive, is faithful to forgive and will wash away all the guilt, shame and regret. When we open our heart (not our mind) to comprehending the truth of this reality, it transforms our lives. We become free; both free to live, love, and laugh again as well as free to give forgiveness to another.

God's Gift of Forgiveness

JESUS said, "Then you will know the truth and the truth will set you free." The TRUTH is, "Take heart my friend; your sins are forgiven. . . .I want you to know that the Son of man has authority on Earth to forgive sins." "Because God made him [Jesus] who had no sin to be sin for us, so that we might become the righteousness of God." Therefore, when "we confess our sins, he is faithful and just and will forgive us our sins and purify us from all unrighteousness." "So if the Son sets you free, you will be free indeed."

John 8:32~Matt. 9:2~II Cor. 5:21~I John 1:9~John 8: 36 Ps. 103:10-14~Neh. 9:17~Ps. 25:11~Psalms 51

Step 1

a. List your regrets or "would-have," "could-have," "should-have" memories:

_____

_____

_____

_____

_____

_____

_____

_____

_____

If you find yourself hesitant to accept God's gift of forgiveness, consider God's heart of joy when humans simply and gratefully receive His gifts. Be aware that by accepting His gift of forgiveness you honor the death of Jesus. He died for your broken heart of guilt, regrets and sin so that you can become whole hearted again.

b. Write your prayer of accepting forgiveness.

Dear Lord, I have _____ and I know it hurt _____.
                (what I did to hurt another)   (the deceased's name)

Today, I want to be free from the guilt and regret I carry with me about this incident. I believe your Scripture in my heart and am willing to let go of trying to cover, hide, lie, or deceive myself or you about the pain I have caused _____.
                (the deceased's name)

When I think of you washing _____ from me, it feels
                (my guilt, regrets, shame, etc. for the actions I chose)

amazing to be clean. I trust you to be my faithful Forgiver. I trust that you do not lie to me about my guilt being thrown to the bottom of the sea. When I am tempted to distrust this healing reality, please remind me of your faithful reality that is evident on the cross when Jesus died for this awful pain. Thank you. (Micah 7:19, I John 1:9, I Cor. 15:3, I Peter 2:24)

Or write your prayer to receive God's forgiveness for the things you listed in Step 1:

Dear Forgiving Father, _____

_____

_____

_____

_____

_____

_____

_____

_____

_____

_____

_____

_____

_____

_____

Step 2

Claim responsibility and apologize for the things you honestly said or did that contributed to the pain in your relationship with the deceased.

a. Write an apology note. Address it to the deceased.

Dear _____

_____

_____

_____

_____

_____

_____

_____

_____

_____

_____

_____

_____

b. Conclude the apology by writing about the assurance that God has forgiven you.

_____

_____

_____

_____

_____

_____

_____

_____

Step 3

a. List the things the deceased or others have done to hurt you:

_____

_____

_____

_____

_____

_____

_____

_____

_____

_____

_____

_____

_____

Forgiving someone who has hurt us **is not**:

- ○ Saying "That's okay."
- ○ Forgetting about it
- ○ Downplaying the harm, hurt, or pain
- ○ Overlooking or diminishing the offence
- ○ Pretending it didn't hurt or took place

Forgiving others is acknowledging the offence and realizing your desire or interest for revenge, hurting back or keeping a grudge.

Forgiving others allows your heart and mind to live free from the imprisonment of the negative feelings that refusing to forgive has caused.

Forgiving releases the offender into the loving heart of God who alone knows how to accurately read the heart of the one who hurt us. By releasing them into God's heart of forgiveness, the cycle of forgiveness can be completed in us. We no longer need to hold our pain or anger as evidence of the wrong that was done to us. It is forgiven and we are set free to move into life, love, and laughter.

b. Write a letter to the deceased or any others you have blamed or been offended by in this death. Forgive them for the pain that they caused you. Let God know that you release responsibility for their behavior and entrust their forgiveness with Him.

Dear _____

_____

_____

_____

_____

_____

_____

_____

_____

_____

_____

_____

_____

_____

_____

_____

_____

_____

_____

_____

_____

_____

_____

_____

_____

_____

_____

_____

_____

CR

ജ

To Grieve or Not to Grieve

There is a time for everything, and a season for every activity under the heavens; . . . a time to weep and a time to laugh.

Ecclesiastes 3:1,4 TNIV

Cycles of emotional relief and intensity are a part of recovery. The ebb and flow of emotions cannot be anticipated fully or controlled when we wish them to leave. Whatever the feelings your grief may be producing, don't run from them, don't fight them. Accept them. Work through your feelings and mix them with what you know to be true about your loss, your healing, and how much God loves you. Remember that God has a plan to bring goodness out of this loss. Trust Him to bring you through the intensity. When you are experiencing relief from the pain, you may feel a sense of guilt. You are encouraged to embrace the relief. Accept the happy times, the smiles, and even the laughter. Our bodies cannot bear the sadness without some kind of relief. Sometimes it is helpful to remind yourself that your loved one would want you to feel happy as often as you can during the hard work of grieving.

From Heart to Hand

What helps me most to accept my grief?
How free or willing am I to be happy?
What would bring me happiness today?

Trusting God Increases Hope

May our Lord Jesus Christ himself and God our Father, who loved us and by his grace gave us eternal encouragement and good hope, encourage your hearts and strengthen you in every good deed and word.

2 Thessalonians 2:16–17 TNIV

 CR _____ ᴓ

Hope! What a refreshing reality hope can bring to us. Hope is real. We hope for what will really take place. We hope for recovery from our pain. We hope for healing of our broken hearts. We hope for Jesus' soon return. We will hold and love our sleeping ones again. Can you see why Romans 8:24 (KJV) reads, "For we are saved in this hope"? Without hope, we would be lost in despair, pain, remorse, regrets, and grief. Hope is another wonderful gift from God that applies to the grieving process as a soothing salve to an infected wound. Allow your mind the relief that is needed by choosing to put your hope in God and His faithfulness to encourage your heart with hope today.

CR _____ ᴓ

From Heart to Hand

What do I hope for?
Develop a definition of hope that brings you comfort.
How can this Scripture comfort me today?

The Privilege Of Suffering

Friends, when life gets really difficult, don't jump to the conclusion that God isn't on the job. Instead, be glad that you are in the very thick of what Christ experienced. This is a spiritual refining process, with glory just around the corner.

I Peter 4:12-13 The Message

The privilege of knowing God and Jesus better is ours through suffering. By facing our emotions and thoughts honestly during our grieving, we are given the opportunity to know God more intimately. We now can understand a little better how Jesus wept over Jerusalem as He faced the reality of losing a nation filled with people He loved. We can understand a little more how the Father must have felt as He watched His Son experience torture and finally a criminal's death. Experiencing suffering can widen our grasp of God's deep love for us. Through the suffering we have tasted, we have only a limited comprehension of God's suffering throughout the ages of this planet. Could it be that heaven's highest honor and most entrusted privilege is to share in the sufferings of God?

From Heart to Hand

How can my suffering help me understand God's suffering?
Can I see suffering as a privilege?
What attributes of God (love, comfort, strength, peace, etc.)
are evident when I contemplate His suffering?

Be Honest

But you desire honesty from the heart, so you can teach me to be wise in my inmost being.

Psalm 51:6 NLT

Grief does not need to be advertised, but an honest account of how you feel should always be given when asked. The key to being honest with others begins first with being honest with yourself. We harm only ourselves when we do not face our emotions honestly and patiently. When we face ourselves openly, we will also be honest with our heavenly Father who already knows how we feel, whether we are admitting our emotions to Him or not. If we deny our feelings, it is very difficult for God to bring healing to them. Today, be honest with yourself. Be honest with others when they ask about your wellbeing. Above all, be honest with God. Let the wisdom of honesty become a full-blooming flower of truth to yourself and others.

From Heart to Hand

What areas of my grief am I hiding from myself, God, and others
(anger, shame, guilt, loneliness, depression, etc.)?
Why might I be afraid to be honest about my pain?
How can my honesty help others to understand the grieving process?

The Need To Blame

I will deliver them from the power of the grave; I will redeem them from death. Where, O death, are your plagues? Where, O grave, is your destruction?

Hosea 13:14 TNIV

Sometimes throughout the seasons of grief, we feel the need to blame someone for the pain we are experiencing and the pain suffered by our loved one. Quite often we find ourselves even blaming God. It might be important to have a little reality check. God did not take your family member or friend. Death did. The consequence of living on a dying planet is that we will all die. Death is the last enemy. However, the blast of the resurrection trumpet will victoriously conquer death. We have a glorious hope that transcends even this earthly reality. We trust that the truth of Jesus' empty grave is the foundation for knowing He will wake us from our sleep of death and be the ultimate conqueror!

From Heart to Hand

Have I been blaming God?
What does this "reality check" do for me?
If God has enough power to resurrect the dead,
could He have enough power to comfort my broken heart today?

Your Tears Are Noticed

You kept track of my every toss and turn through the sleepless nights, each tear entered in your ledger, each ache written in your book.

Psalms 56:8 The Message

Your tears, whether a man or woman, are not a sign of weakness or shame. They are a natural response to pain. They may be a representation of your love or deep pain for the loss of what can never be recovered. It is very unfortunate that our culture does not welcome our tears. We are taught at an early age to hold in our watery sadness. Little boys and men are especially misguided to swallow their pain. Fortunately, modern science is discovering that tears actually flush the body of certain toxins that would otherwise not find release. So, if you tear easily, consider yourself blessed and know that you are actually participating in healthy grieving. If tears seem absent please consider that they are intended by God to help release the physical residue of bereavement. Your tears matter to God. He knows when they fall and the pain they represent. Your tears are safe in His presence.

From Heart to Hand

How does the above Scripture bring me comfort today?
Ideas to encourage your tears: Think of your loved one, breathe slowly
and deeply, welcome sad feelings, be alone where you
can be vocal as you put your feelings on paper.
What do my tears mean to me?

"Why?" Part One

*About three in the afternoon Jesus cried out in a loud voice, "Eli, Eli, lema sabachthani?" (Which means, "My God, my God, **why** have you forsaken me?)*

Matthew 27:46 TNIV

Why do these things happen: death, murder, accidents, terminal illness, violence, crime & suffering? Brilliant philosophers and theologians have explored these questions that spring from our broken hearted souls. I too asked the "Why?" questions at the time of our son's death. While I am no theologian, I can say I have been in the process of personally knowing God for nearly 45 years. Today, we are encouraged as we remember that even Jesus asked the "Why?" question when he hung in physical and spiritual agony on the cross. He knows and understands our searing questions. He has experienced the sense of utter abandonment so that we could be strengthened by accepting that he took our deepest and most confusing grief upon himself. By doing this for us we can receive his reassurance and comfort.

From Heart to Hand

How does it help me to think about Jesus asking "Why?"
What are my most pressing "Why?" questions?
How can I be at peace even if I might not
understand "Why?" this side of Heaven?

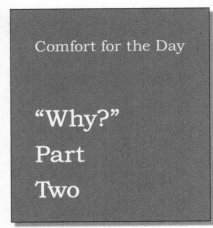

Comfort for the Day

"Why?" Part Two

I have told you these things, so that in me you may have peace. In this world you will have trouble. But take heart! I have overcome the world.

John 16:33 TNIV

The answer to our grieving, screaming cries of "Why?" are found in a brief insight that Jesus gave the night of his arrest. As you read the verse above, what did Jesus say about living on this planet? Yes, we will have trouble here. Last I checked we each have an address that is associated with Planet Earth. "This world," as Jesus said, is full of trouble. He knew it from his personal experience with being misunderstood, bullied, scoffed at, attempted stoning, and finally crucified. He knows it is unsafe to live on this troubled world. He even knows why it is full of trouble. An enemy of the Kingdom of Love has captured us in a web of pain and suffering. But Jesus offers us His peace while we live on this crazy hurting planet. We don't even have to have all the answers to our questions. We can simply embrace His promise. His peace is real. It comes from Him and you can have it now.

From Heart to Hand

When I think that Jesus knows how I feel, how does that help me?
What encourages me to accept his promises of peace?
Where do I need peace most in my grieving experience?

Ask "How?" Instead of "Why?"

I cry out to God; yes, I shout. Oh, that God would listen to me! When I was in deep trouble, I searched for the Lord. All night long I prayed, with hands lifted toward heaven, but my soul was not comforted. Has the Lord rejected me forever? Will he never again be kind to me? Is his unfailing love gone forever? Have his promises permanently failed? But then I recall all you have done, O LORD; I remember your wonderful deeds of long ago. They are constantly in my thoughts. I cannot stop thinking about your mighty works. O God, your ways are holy. Is there any god as mighty as you?

Psalm 77:1–2, 7–8, 11–13 NLT

It is human nature to ask questions. We begin early in life asking "why" questions. Every parent can remember the many "why" questions that they could not adequately answer their children because of the child's limited ability to understand the situation. We are God's beloved children, and there are some "why" questions that we cannot perceive the answers to. God is not impatient with our questioning. The urge to ask still remains, so try asking "how." How is God still in control? How will my pain go away? How can I trust Him with all my questions? How does this death bring Him honor and glory? May you trust God today with all your difficult questions.

From Heart to Hand

Right now, I view God as . . .
How does this scripture comfort my needs today?
How can I practice patience as I wait for God's answers to my questions?

Okay Lord, "How?"

Meanwhile, the moment we get tired in the waiting, God's Spirit is right alongside helping us along. If we don't know how or what to pray, it doesn't matter. He does our praying in and for us, making prayer out of our wordless sighs, our aching groans. He knows us far better than we know ourselves, knows our pregnant condition, and keeps us present before God. That's why we can be so sure that every detail in our lives of love for God is worked into something good.

Romans 8:26–28 The Message

How can good come from your loss? You may not be able to answer that question, but God can. It is His responsibility to make good out of your painful situation. Take God at His word. He will refresh you with His Spirit and bring new understanding to your heart. God can and will work good from your loss. As you put your confidence in Him, others will see the good coming through you that God has promised. Can others see you as a grieving person who is trusting and waiting on God to answer your questions? Do they observe a peace that the world does not know in grief? Through your example, others can be encouraged to face their losses with trust in God also.

From Heart to Hand

How has God already brought about some good through my loss?
Reflect on the verse for this day and put it on paper.
What part of my broken heart still needs to be entrusted to God's healing?

Grace to Match The Need

Each time he said, "My grace is all you need. My power works best in weakness." So now I am glad to boast about my weaknesses, so that the power of Christ can work through me.

2 Corinthians 12:9 NLT

But to each one of us grace was given according to the measure of Christ's gift."

Ephesians 4:7 NKJV

The paralyzing effect of loss may leave us feeling helpless, hopeless, and even incapable of performing daily duties. At times the pain is so intense we feel as if we can't make it through another day. It is at these times that our friend Jesus comes to us saying, "I know all about your weakness and pain. In fact, in your greatest point of pain, my strength is limitlessly available to you. My grace is my ability to do for you what you cannot do for yourself. Do you trust me to meet your need?" We are helpless to control the path of grief. Yet with God's grace to do for us what we are unable to do for ourselves, we can be strengthened with assurance that the power of Christ is at work through our weaknesses. His gift comes from the riches of eternity. We have all we need when we trust Him with our weakness.

From Heart to Hand

In what areas of my grieving do I need God's grace?
What is my understanding or definition of grace?
How do these Scriptures comfort me today?

Anticipating the Firsts

Therefore do not worry about tomorrow, for tomorrow will worry about itself. Each day has enough trouble of its own.

Matthew 6:34 TNIV

As we live through the seasons of grief, we are sometimes overcome with fearful anticipation of how we will handle the first anniversaries of the year: the first birthday and holidays without our loved one. Please trust a fellow traveler who has gone ahead of you a bit when I say that the anticipation is usually worse than the significant day or event. Intentionally prepare to honor the life of your loved one during the seasons of the first year. It is one of the best ways to harness the fear and put it to work on your behalf. You might plant a tree, prepare a special recipe, write in this journal, or invite friends or family to join you in a special tribute or memorial. Please remember that the intentional work you do will make it easier the next year and the next and the next … Jesus counsels us to live the seasons of grief just one day at a time. Don't worry about tomorrow.

From Heart to Hand

How could making plans about the "firsts" help me?
What significant events have seemed worse than they really were?
Who could help me plan a meaningful way to remember my loved one?

The Despair of Sadness

Save me, O God, for the floodwaters are up to my neck. Deeper and deeper I sink into the mire; I can't find a foothold. I am in deep water, and the floods overwhelm me. I am exhausted from crying for help; my throat is parched. My eyes are swollen with weeping, waiting for my God to help me.

Psalm 69:1–3 NLT

The despair of sadness is the inability to be happy or comforted. This condition may be caused by physical factors as well as spiritual ones. Lack of rest, limited exercise along with a poor diet can cause deep physical fatigue, thus causing a very real emotional fatigue. STOP! Rest, sleep, eat right, cancel appointments, and call on the Lord who will always hear your cry for help. When the disciples on the storm-tossed sea cried out, "Oh, Lord, save us, we are going to die," they were in their darkest despair. Never is that plea for help unanswered. Jesus was there with those disciples the whole time. He is with you, too. Jesus promises to never leave us. He shelters us under His warm downy wings and protects us from our own fears. Keep your mind focused on His healing and faithfulness toward you. The despair of sadness will lift as you focus your thoughts on eternal realities. Be patient. Allow God to fill you with courage to trust His timing in restoring His joy within you.

From Heart to Hand

What thoughts of Heaven and eternity bring me the greatest joy?
What changes in my daily routine can I make that will help me feel better?
What adjustments am I willing to make to move past the despair?

Fear in Grieving

Cast all your anxiety on him because he cares for you.

1 Peter 5:7 TNIV

If this is your first experience with grieving the death of someone important to you, you might be aware that you are now traveling in unfamiliar emotional and physical territory. Fear often accompanies the unknown which only adds to the anxiety of grieving. Healthy grievers understand that their fears are normal AND they take action to trust those fears to the One who can pacify them with His peace. The critical step is to be honest about our fears. Acknowledge them. Face them. Then throw them down. Throw them down at the feet of Jesus who alone has ability to deal with each one in His perfect time. At the same time, He comes close to you with assurance and peace because He cares for you!

From Heart to Hand

List your fears, then write the name JESUS over them as an act of faith that Jesus knows how to take care of every fear you are currently experiencing.
Write how much God cares for you.
Where do I see evidences of God's caring for me?

CR

છ

Grief's Anger

When you are angry, don't let it carry you into sin. Don't let the sun set with anger in your heart or give the devil room to work.

Ephesians 4:26,27 The Voice

ᘓ_____ᘔ

Anger is a natural grief experience. It is among the emotional seasons including; despair, sadness, depression, guilt, remorse, etc. When anger overtakes us, it might be helpful to understand that it is simply another emotional season we are *living through.* Journaling about our anger is the safest way to process it and release it to the healing intentions of God. When we deny the anger, pretend that we are not angry, or hurt others with it, we need to STOP and do our grief work on paper. As you write about your anger, you might discover several targets. Be fully angry at each target on paper. Deal with it daily when needed. The wisdom in this Scripture urges us to be truthful, and make healthy choices that will discontinue hurting our hearts and the hearts of others.

ᘓ_____ᘔ

From Heart to Hand

Who am I angry with today? Make a list. Be completely honest with yourself and God. Write about releasing the anger into the strength of God's power.
What do I know about the character of God and how
His kingdom operates that will help me let go of my anger?

Patience with the Process

Wait on the Lord; be of good courage, and He shall strengthen your heart; wait, I say, on the Lord!

Psalm 27:14 NKJV

ᘓ_____ ᘒ

Be patient with yourself. If you find you are unable to do all the activities you used to or that your physical energy level is limited, pace yourself. Do not push. This is part of physical grief (review pages 14-20). God is the source of all healing and He will heal you in His time. Impatience increases anxiety. You have enough pain, worry, and trouble in each day so be patient with yourself through the grieving seasons. As you cooperate patiently, you will notice God's faithfulness and evidence of your healing.

ᘓ_____ ᘒ

From Heart to Hand

What areas in my life am I most impatient about?
How can I enact my trust in God's timing for my recovery?
How can this Scripture comfort me today?

Grief is Hard Work

Dear friends, don't be surprised at the fiery trials you are going through, as if something strange were happening to you.

1 Peter 4:12 NLT

ℭ℞_____℘℆

Death is often the beginning point of pain for those who remain. The first year will be filled with all those painful "firsts" without your loved one/s. Things that you think would be too painful will be easier if they are faced early. The earlier you return to those familiar places, the earlier you face the holidays, the earlier you visit the grave, the easier it will be. Being intentional takes effort and follow through. Grieving is difficult work. We often struggle with the awkwardness of starting to live again. It does become easier. Please believe that, especially when you choose to do your grief work each day. Pay attention to your heart, and journal about it. And when it is not easy, look back to remember all that God has already done to support you along the journey. Lean into the arms of God. Trust His strength to grace you for the work of grieving. He is the strongest and most comforting of companions to be with you as you revisit the most painful memories.

ℭ℞_____℘℆

From Heart to Hand

What emotions or barriers are hindering me
from facing some of the "firsts?"
What do I need to remember about God that
will help me be intentional about my grieving?
What is my plan to prepare for the next "first?"

Contentment in Uncertainty

For I have learned to be content whatever the circumstances. I know what it is to be in need, and I know what it is to have plenty. I have learned the secret of being content in any and every situation, whether well fed or hungry, whether living in plenty or in want. I can do all this through him who gives me strength.

Philippians 4:11–13 TNIV

Some days are filled with overwhelming loneliness over the absence of your loved one. Take the time and make the effort to look around and notice the people who are nearest to you. These friends and family could never take the place of the loss in your life, but they can bring you much contentment. Allow their care and love for you to soothe the emptiness. Lean into God's strength to refocus your thinking. The childhood tune that goes, *"count your many blessings, name them one by one"* is good advice for today. Your day is filled with unrecognized blessings that God has given just for you. Ask God to open your eyes to see the wonder of an opening rosebud, the splendor of a sunset, the comfort from a friend, and the joy in a child's smile.

From Heart to Hand

What unrecognized blessings do I need to notice today?
Make a list of supportive and caring family and friends.
How can I apply the message from today's Scripture?

Death is but A Sleep

We believe that Jesus died and rose again, and so we believe that God will bring with Jesus those who have fallen asleep in him.

1 Thessalonians 4:14 TNIV

There is comfort in knowing our deceased loved ones are "sleeping." God safely holds their life and will reunite that life to their immortal bodies at His second coming. Our loved ones are not in a state of consciousness now. They know no pain, pleasure, or passing of time. Death is but an instant to them. While it is painful to think about the decay of their body, the Bible assures us that the elements of humanity only return to their original state. "In the sweat of your face you shall eat bread till you return to the ground, for out of it you were taken; for dust you are, and to dust you shall return." (Genesis 3:19 NKJV). According to Jesus, we will receive immortal bodies at His return. Then we will, all together, go with Him to meet our heavenly Father.

From Heart to Hand

How does the "sleep" of death comfort me today?
What can I learn about God's character when I consider that
my loved one sleeps rather than is conscious at this moment?
What do I anticipate when I consider seeing my resurrected loved one?

Accept God's Comfort

Praise be to the God and Father of our Lord Jesus Christ, the Father of compassion and the God of all comfort, who comforts us in all our troubles, so that we can comfort those in any trouble with the comfort we ourselves receive from God.

2 Corinthians 1:3–4 TNIV

To insist on suffering in our grief when God's comfort is available is like being a starving beggar refusing warm, delicious food. Sometimes our self-pity parties get in the way of accepting God's perfect comfort for our current need. God's desire to comfort is as sure as His love for you. No one understands you like Jesus. He knows the depth of your need mentally, emotionally, and physically. He is your best and most constant source of support, understanding, and comfort. Our need cannot outweigh God's strength, comfort, wisdom, understanding, and love! We are safe when we welcome His embrace, crying until we come to perfect rest in His strength. Exercise your faith in His faithfulness toward you and allow His comfort to meet your need today.

From Heart to Hand

What picture comes to mind when I think of God comforting me?
What kind of comfort do I need from God today?
For further reading, see the additional Bible verses
of God's comfort on pages 148-149

Pain and Suffering are not Forever

For our light and momentary troubles are achieving for us an eternal glory that far outweighs them all. So we fix our eyes not on what is seen, but on what is unseen, since what is seen is temporary, but what is unseen is eternal.

2 Corinthians 4:17–18 TNIV

How easy it is to become consumed in our grief! It encompasses every part of our being. At times it seems eternal, yet it is only temporary. It takes just the slightest degree of our will to choose to look up. Allow your mind the relief of dwelling on the eternal realities. This is not a denial of your loss, your pain or your suffering. Rather it provides a brief and welcome relief form living under the "shadow of the valley of death." Yes, your grief, your loss, is real, but it is only temporary. Eternity and its realities are forever and ever and ever. The imagination can allow our tired emotions the rest they need while filling our minds with mental pictures of heaven and an earth made new, free of pain and suffering. Imagine the reunion with our loved ones, and most importantly, a wonderfully uninterrupted relationship with God. May this be your experience today.

From Heart to Hand

What are my most imaginative thoughts about eternity?
Write a prayer for God's help to keep my mind on eternal realities.
What happens when I consider that my suffering will have an end?

The Perfect Heart Reader

Will not the Judge of all the earth do right?

Genesis 18:25 TNIV

If you are struggling with thoughts about your sleeping loved one's eternal life, you are not alone. This is particularly true for families that must deal with mental illness, suicide, or death caused by substance abuse. At the funeral or memorial service, many positive attributes and characteristics of your loved one may have been given. But something may still nag at you about their eternal destiny. The good news is that God alone is the judge. He is the only one who knows and understands everyone's heart. His judgment is consistent with His character. He determines everyone's final outcome through his love, mercy, righteousness, wisdom, and truth. He makes no mistakes. He knows if we would be happy or unhappy living eternally in His kingdom of love. Praise God we don't need to carry the responsibility of judgment! Let it go.

From Heart to Hand

In what areas have I passed judgment on my loved one?
How does knowing that God is the judge comfort me today?
If I have fears of God's judgment, are they based on
the truth of God's character or my own feelings?

Knowing God's Will

For it is my Father's will that all who see his Son and believe in him should have eternal life. I will raise them up at the last day."

John 6:40 NLT

CR _____ ℰ⊃

Sometimes we think God wishes harm to us or others. According to Scripture, God sent His Son into this world to save us, not to harm us or condemn us. The Father's will is for all who believe in His Son to have the assurance of eternal life. Because Jesus didn't stay dead, He has authority and the ability to raise from the dead all who will be happy to live in His kingdom of love. Remember, we don't know the heart of another, so allow God to determine if your loved one had a heart for God. If someone we loved rests in death, we can be grateful they do not have to struggle any more on this difficult planet. Is there really anything so bad about laying a loved one down for a long nap until Jesus comes to raise them from their sleep of death? His promise is sure! He will raise them up on that last day.

CR _____ ℰ⊃

From Heart to Hand

How do Jesus' words comfort me today?
How confident am I of God's assurance for my own eternal life?
How can I put my trust in God for the final outcome of my loved one?

Grieving With Hope

Brothers and sisters, we do not want you to be uninformed about those who sleep in death, so that you do not grieve like the rest, who have no hope. For the Lord himself will come down from heaven, with a loud command, with the voice of the archangel and with the trumpet call of God, and the dead in Christ will rise first. After that, we who are still alive and are left will be caught up together with them in the clouds to meet the Lord in the air. And so we will be with the Lord forever.

I Thessalonians 4:13, 16–18 TNIV

The Bible does not say that we should not grieve, but it does say that we should not grieve as the world does, without hope. Hope is a wonderful agent of healing. Realistic hope is based on the reality of God's love and goodwill for our lives. He can bring light to a dark day and courage to us when we feel despair. We hope for what we do not yet have: comfort for the pain, meaning for the loss, healing of relationships, and answers to the questions. It is also natural to hope for the great reunion when our sleeping loved ones will be resurrected. We hope for a land without fear, pain, or tears. The Bible is the best place to search for hope. It will be found in its pages, for it is filled with promises to instill hope in our lives.

From Heart to Hand

What are my greatest fears: isolation, financial loss, pain, illness?
How can hope be an agent for my healing?
Reflect on the verses on hope found on pages 148-149.

In His Time

Yet God has made everything beautiful for its own time. He has planted eternity in the human heart, but even so, people cannot see the whole scope of God's work from beginning to end.

Ecclesiastes 3:11 NLT

An Expression often offered to hurting, grieving people is, "Time will heal." While it is well intended, it does not always leave us feeling encouraged. Our internal thinking might answer back with these thoughts, *"How much time? I'm exhausted. The waiting is so hard."* Time only puts distance between the death and the present. While it is true that God *uses* the means of time to heal our broken hearts and wounded emotions, it is **God** who does the healing. In His time, He will heal and bring restoration and even recovery. He knows each of us and understands the best method and time frame in which to bring about our healing. Already there may be recent experiences that affirm God's use of time in your healing process. In the future, look for evidences of His timing and healing. Trust Him and allow your stress to rest.

From Heart to Hand

What evidence of God's timing have I already seen in my grief recovery?
How does choosing to trust God's timing for my recovery help me today?
What season of grief am I currently experiencing:
Winter, Spring, Summer or Fall?

God is More Creative Than Your Pain

So if you are suffering in a manner that pleases God, keep on doing what is right, and trust your lives to the God who created you, for he will never fail you.

1 Peter 4:19 NLT

To all who mourn in Israel, he will give a crown of beauty for ashes, a joyous blessing instead of mourning, festive praise instead of despair. In their righteousness, they will be like great oaks that the LORD has planted for his own glory.

Isaiah 61:3 NLT

When waves of grieving despair beat against you, turn to your faithful Creator, God. He is so creative that no matter how black and ugly your situation, He can make something beautiful from it. Let me illustrate. The powers of darkness have violently heaved an enormous mountain of scrap metal and garbage in the middle of your path. You are overwhelmed with suffering. The ugliness and pain is all you can see. But there is Someone who is so powerful and creative, that He can turn this trash heap into something absolutely beautiful. That Someone is Jesus! He knows from His own experience what suffering is like. He also created this world and all its beauty out of nothing by speaking the world into existence. He certainly has the power and creativity to take the difficult circumstances in your grieving experience and turn them into something very good. Let him exchange your ashes for beauty. Look for Him to "repurpose" your mourning into something of magnificent beauty, joy, and praise.

From Heart to Hand

Contemplate God's creative powers as seen in nature.
How have I recognized God's creativity even in my darkness and pain?
What beauty is coming from my situation?

Cooperate with the Physician

When Jesus saw him lying there and learned that he had been in this condition for a long time, he asked him, "Do you want to get well?"

John 5:6 TNIV

What an odd question for a physician to ask a patient, "Do you want to be well again?" Yet your heavenly Physician is asking you that question today. The man in the Bible story replied to Jesus by telling Him about the circumstances that were keeping him from being able to get well, but that wasn't what Jesus wanted to know. He simply wanted to know if the man really desired to be made whole again. So Jesus responded by telling the man to get up and walk, and this time the man rose immediately and complied with Jesus' command. The Physician was in his presence and realizing that, the man quickly cooperated. There are things you can do today to cooperate with your heavenly Physician. The first step is to be willing to give away your heavy burden of grief. Are you willing to be happy again? Rather than telling the Physician all about the reasons why you need to keep your broken heart, begin cooperating today and watch how He will tenderly and lovingly restore you.

From Heart to Hand

Revisit the sections found on pages 5-13 to evaluate
my use of emotional healing remedies.
What attitudes might be hindering me from using some
of the physical healing tools? (pages 14-20)
Which of the eight proven ways of cooperating with God's healing
have been most beneficial to me? (page 18)

Becoming a New You

This means that anyone who belongs to Christ has become a new person. The old life is gone; a new life has begun!

2 Corinthians 5:17 NLT

Many months after the death of my son, I began to wonder, "Who am I?" A part of me had died, and it seemed I would never be the same person again. That bothered me for a long while until I realized and accepted that it was okay not to be the same person I used to be. Because of my encounter with death, I interacted with life differently. Due to my experience with death, loss, suffering, and grief I realized that it was my choice to allow my new life to become handicapped or to become enhanced. With Jesus as my personal friend through it all, I challenged myself to become a better person because of my loss. My old life was gone. Every morning I am a new creation by God's healing grace. You can be, too.

From Heart to Hand

What changes in myself do I notice?
Which of these changes are positive?
How can I become a better person through my
experience with grief and God's healing?

CR

છ

Comfort Others

He comforts us in all our troubles so that we can comfort others. When they are troubled, we will be able to give them the same comfort God has given us.

2 Corinthians 1:4 NLT

ℭ℟_____℮℧

Reaching out to comfort someone else is excellent therapy for our

own grief recovery. Through your pain and confidence in God's healing for you, you can come alongside another grieving person and be supportive of them in their anguish. The shared experience of loss connects you to each other in a way that nothing else can. It feels good to help another. Passing on encouragement and hope is a way of living as a citizen of God's eternal kingdom of love. While God is willing to give us everything we need, He is honored when we pass on to others the comfort and encouragement we have received from Him.

ℭ℟_____℮℧

From Heart to Hand

Who do I know that needs my comfort today?
What would be the best means to reach out to another:
telephone, letter, e-mail, in person, etc.?
How well am I accepting God's comfort in my own experience?

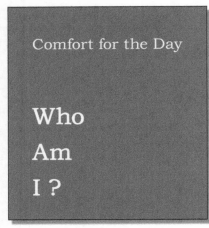

Comfort for the Day

Who Am I?

For I am about to do something new. See, I Have already begun! Do you not see it? I will make a pathway through the wilderness. I will create rivers in the dry wasteland.

Isaiah 43:19 NLT

❦_____❧

As healing takes place, you may begin to question, "Who am I? I am not the same person I used to be. Part of me is missing. I am afraid to do the things I used to do. How much responsibility can I safely take on? Will I ever feel genuinely happy again?" I call this experience "re-entry." There is awkwardness in your emotions and your actions. There may be a hesitancy to meet new people for fear they will not truly understand you for they did not know the precious person you lost to death. These thoughts and questions can be comforted by the realization that God wants to make you a new person. You have suffered a terrible wound, but your loss can become your greatest asset. You can become a better, more caring person who is willing to be involved with a hurting, troubled world. Trust that God will provide a clear path in the wilderness of sorrow and rivers of refreshing in your desert of pain.

❦_____❧

From Heart to Hand

What new ways of thinking or living am I experiencing right now?
What "wasteland" experiences have I gone through that
will help me support others in their grief recovery?
How does this Scripture comfort me today?

I will not leave you as orphans;
I will come to you. . . . because I
live, you also will live.

John 14:18–19 TNIV

Loneliness

Hurting, grieving people are often isolated and left alone in their grief. The loneliness is nearly unbearable and only magnifies the pain. Try taking the initiative to put others at ease with your grief. This relieves your friends who otherwise might find themselves avoiding you because of their own fears about emotional pain. One benefit in taking the initiative to speak to others first is that it will help them to understand grief in general and your personal grief recovery process in particular. If for some reason you are misunderstood in your attempts to reach out to others, be comforted in knowing that Jesus is your friend who will never abandon you.

From Heart to Hand

When feeling lonely, how does this Scripture help me?
How have I made it easier or more difficult for
my friends to relieve my loneliness?
How can I live today remembering that I am not
an orphan nor abandoned by God?

One Day at A Time

Give your entire attention to what God is doing right now, and don't get worked up about what may or may not happen tomorrow. God will help you deal with whatever hard things come up when the time comes.

Matthew 6:34 The Message

Although plans must be made for the future, now is a very good time to take life only one day at a time. That does not mean that all activity stops while you wait on your healing and recovery. No. It means that you are free to live to the fullest each moment that is given to you, one day at a time. Living one day at a time releases the anxiety you might be carrying about tomorrow's events. Also, as you embrace God's forgiveness, living one day at a time releases the burden of guilt and regrets from yesterday. All we have is this day. Yesterday is gone and forgiven! Tomorrow never comes! TODAY you may live with trust in God to supply all your needs. How grateful you can be that God only gives you one day at a time!

From Heart to Hand

Do I find myself living or thinking most frequently
in yesterday, today, or tomorrow?
What can I do to help myself live just one day at a time?
How would my attitude change if I began to live in the present?

CR

૭૦

Letting Go

There is a time for everything, and a season for every activity under the heavens: a time to be born and a time to die., . . .

Ecclesiastes 3:1–2 TNIV

❦───❦

Death is a temporary interruption of a relationship. Yet we fight, we resist, we long to hold on. Is it the loss of control and fear that drives our reluctance to release our hearts to healing? Maybe we don't understand what is meant by "letting go." Letting go means allowing the relationship to rest. A real relationship takes at least two people. When one person dies, that relationship is interrupted. No one says it is easy to rest the love in our hearts. According to today's Scripture, there is a time to live and there is a time to die. There is a time to rest and let go and there is a time to process the healing. Letting go or resting the relationship hurts, but pain is an indicator of a wound that is healing. How much better it is to experience pain instead of numbness! How much better it is to face the reality of our emotions and memories than to close our heart's door! How much better to allow rest to take the place of clinging to what we cannot have right now!

❦───❦

From Heart to Hand

What do I need to let go of?
Can I let go a little at a time or would it be best to completely let go?
What do I want to hold on to?
Suggestion for writing: Write a "letting go" letter.
Include your emotions and plans for a hope-filled future.

Comfort for the Day

Constructive or Destructive Memories

Friends, don't get me wrong: by no means do I count myself an expert in all of this, but I've got my eye on the goal, where God is beckoning us onward—to Jesus. I'm off and running and I'm not turning back.

Philippians 3:12–14 The Message

Time, wisdom, and patience are the recovery tools to apply to your memories. What memories need to be let go of and which ones need to be retained? This question is especially significant for those whose loss is surrounded by violence or prolonged suffering. Let's face it—death is ugly. It is healing to let the ugly memories vanish with the past. It is healing to accept God's forgiveness and to extend that forgiveness toward others in our past or present situation. It is also healing to retain the sweet memories. Keep fresh in your memory the evidence of God's faithfulness to you through your season of loss and healing. But the best frame of mind is to keep thinking forward toward the goal of living each day with the God whose plans for healing are beyond your imagination.

From Heart to Hand

What memory do I want to keep fresh in my thoughts today?
Do I need to think about forgiveness differently?
What memory am I willing to let go of?

Suggestion for writing: On a separate piece of paper, write all your destructive memories, give them to God in prayer, and then destroy the paper. In this book, record your constructive memories, giving thanks to God for those precious recollections of your loved one and God's faithfulness to you.

Then
We
Will See
Face to Face

I heard a voice thunder from the Throne: "Look! Look! God has moved into the neighborhood, making his home with men and women! They're his people, he's their God. He'll wipe every tear from their eyes. Death is gone for good—tears gone, crying gone, pain gone—all the first order of things gone" The Enthroned continued, "Look! I'm making everything new. Write it all down—each word dependable and accurate."

Revelation 21:3–5 The Message

Thinking and talking about eternal realities is one of the best choices you can make for your recovery. Let your imagination grow and develop as you contemplate what the above Scripture is saying. The Bible says, "Therefore comfort each other with these words" (1 Thessalonians 4:18) KJV. "These words" refer to Jesus' second coming and the resurrection of the dead. Together you and your loved one will meet each other to live eternally. Close your eyes and imagine the feelings, sights, and sounds of that moment. Jesus' return is a reality. Heaven is a reality. If you are uncertain about the eternal security of your sleeping loved one, please know you can safely trust that decision to your loving Heavenly Father. What a day to look forward to when God wipes your tears away, and you will never again experience pain or suffering!

From Heart to Hand

What emotions am I feeling today?
How does this Scripture comfort me today?
How can I trust God with the eternal outcome of my loved one?
*Suggestion for writing: Let your imagination
expand as you contemplate your future reunions.*

Living With a Healed Heart

> . . . . *a time to heal,*
> . . . . *a time to build,*
> . . . . *a time to laugh,*
> . . . . *a time to dance,*
>
> Ecclesiastes 3:3,4

There comes a time . . . . a time to embrace your healing. This new season slowly emerges from the ashes of loss. Once again we can taste and see the beauty and loveliness of life. The constant shadow of our grief-storm has ended. We wake up to healing. We have worked through the grief. We have grown, changed and adjusted to the empty space left by our loved one. We consider that stepping forward into the joy of living is indeed a tribute to the deceased. Our life is healthier. We are more compassionate and patient. We find ourselves less bothered with minor inconveniences because the really big issues of loss have put the little things into perspective. We are a little wiser and quicker to forgive. This new season is the time to live out our healing, to build, laugh, and dance once again. This new season is ours because God has faithfully brought healing to our broken hearts and now we say, "Thank you, Lord!"

From Heart to Hand

What are some of the differences I am noticing in my life experiences?
Who do I know that needs encouragement to do
their grief work? How will I help them?
Suggested writing: Write a "Thank you" note to
God for His healing work in your life.

Extra Pages for Journaling

CR _____

_____

_____

_____

_____

_____

_____

_____

_____

_____

_____

_____

_____

_____

_____

_____

_____

_____

_____

_____

_____

_____

_____

_____

_____

_____

_____

_____

CR

80

Notes ~ Quotes ~ Memories ~ Sketches

For some, putting pencil to paper without words is a healing exercise. These pages are included just for you. When words can't be expressed, sometimes shapes and forms, shades and contrast provide an outlet for our pain, sorrow or questions. Extra lines are provided for other notes, quotes or memories that you want to have easy access to as you work through your grieving.

Sketches ~ Notes ~ Quotes ~ Memories

Sketches ~ Notes ~ Quotes ~ Memories

Sketches ~ Notes ~ Quotes ~ Memories

Sketches ~ Notes ~ Quotes ~ Memories

Sketches ~ Notes ~ Quotes ~ Memories

Sketches ~ Notes ~ Quotes ~ Memories

Sketches ~ Notes ~ Quotes ~ Memories

Sketches ~ Notes ~ Quotes ~ Memories

Sketches ~ Notes ~ Quotes ~ Memories

CB

ജ

❧ God's Words to Comfort You ❧

God's Comfort
Psalm 94:17–19
Isaiah 49:13
Isaiah 61:1–3
Mathew 5:4
John 14:16, 18, 26
2 Corinthians 1:2–4
2 Thessalonians 2:16
Revelation 21:4

God's Constant Presence
Deuteronomy 31:8
Psalm 23
Isaiah 41:10
Isaiah 43:2
Isaiah 54:10
Isaiah 58:20
Matthew 28:20
John 14:16
Romans 8:35–39
Hebrews 13:5

Trusting God
Psalm 4:5
Psalm 31
Psalm 50:7–11
Psalm 56:3-4
Proverbs 3:5–6
Jeremiah 9:23–24

Healing for Emotions
Psalm 147:3
Isaiah 40:31
Isaiah 61:1

Philippians 4:19
1 Peter 5:7

Forgiveness
Psalm 103:11–14
Psalm 86:4–7
Psalm 25:15–18
Matthew 9:1–8
2 Corinthians 2:7
1 John 1:9

Rest & Peace
Psalm 4:8
Isaiah 26:3–4
Isaiah 30:15
Matthew 11:28
John 14:27
Philippians 4:7

Time
Psalm 31:15
Ecclesiastes 3:1–11
Romans 8:28

God's Help
Psalm 57:1–3
Psalm 119:49–50
Hebrews 4:16
Philippians 4:19
1 Corinthians 10:13

Real Hope
Psalm 31:24
Psalm 43:5

Jeremiah 31:15–16
Romans 15:4, 13
Titus 1:2 & 2:13

Comfort Each Other
2 Corinthians 2:7
1 Thessalonians 5:14
Philippians 2:1–2
Colossians 2:2–3

Honest with God
Psalm 6:6–9
Psalm 51:6
Psalm 69:1–3
Psalm 77:2,6,7,11–13
1 Timothy 2:2

Suffering's Purposes
Isaiah 48:10
Romans 8:17,18
2 Corinthians 1:5 & 4:17–18
1 Peter 4:12,13,19
Philippians 3:10

The New You
Psalm 71:20–21
Psalm 51:10–12
Isaiah 43:18-19
Romans 8:28
2 Corinthians 5:17

Death is Sleep
Psalm 115:17
Ecclesiastes 9:5–6
Daniel 12:2
John 11:11,14
1 Thessalonians 4:13–14

1 Corinthians 15:51,53
Revelation 21:14

The Resurrection
John 6:39-40 & 11:25
1 Corinthians 15:12-26
Thessalonians 4:13–18
Revelation 20:6

Victory over Death
Isaiah 25:8
Hosea 13:14
Revelation 14:3 & 21:4

 # Resources

For additional grief support, visit our blogs at www.comfortfortheday.com

Keep regularly encouraged by following *Comfort for the Day* on Facebook

Bring Steve and Karen into your home to coach you through your grief in this dynamic online video course. Karen helps you learn about your best options for healthy grief in each of the 25 videos and downloads. Through stories, up to date grief information and Scripture, Karen's personal and clear wisdom will guide you with healthy grief options. View the videos at your convenience in the privacy of your own home.

Order your online video course at
courses.comfortfortheday.com

Comfort for the Day Seminars
Invite Steve and Karen to present a grief education workshop
at your church or place of work

Karen's interactive, engaging, and insightful speaking style brings her audience into the heart of genuine grief support. Learn to reduce your awkwardness about what to say or do for a grieving friend. Discover new ways to confidently comfort others. Teaching both grievers and comforters, Steve and Karen offer real help for hurting hearts and those who comfort them as they speak to groups about healthy grief choices. Steve specializes in speaking to men about their unique grief.

Contact us at
steve@griefoptions.com ~ 530-878-5013
P.O. Box 7199 Auburn CA 95604